# 44

# THE LEGACY

44th President

# OF BARACK

of the United States of America

# OBAMA

# CONTENTS

★ ★ ★

# CHANGE

*Will not come*

## IF WE WAIT FOR SOME OTHER PERSON OR SOME OTHER TIME.
### WE ARE THE ONES WE'VE BEEN WAITING FOR.

——— *We are the* ———

## ❧ CHANGE ❧

that we seek

◆ ◆ ◆ ◆ ◆ ◆ ◆ ◆ ◆

**President Barack Obama**

# EARLY LIFE

Known today as the 44th United States President, Barack Obama was born in Honolulu, Hawaii, on August 4, 1961. His parents were both students at the University of Hawaii at the time of his birth. Ann Dunham, Obama's mother, was born to Madelyn and Stanley Dunham on November 29, 1942, in Wichita, Kansas. She was a gifted student and received both a bachelor's degree and a master's degree in anthropology from the University of Hawaii at Manoa, where she met Obama's father. Barack Obama Sr. was born June 18, 1936 in Rachuonyo District, Kenya. Much like Dunham, Barack Obama Sr. was also a talented intellectual who attended the University of Hawaii after being selected for a special scholarship program. He eventually obtained a bachelor's degree in economics from the university, and a master's of economics from Harvard University. Ann Dunham and Barack Obama Sr. married on February 2, 1961.

Obama's parents divorced in in 1964, and Obama was primarily raised first by his mother and stepfather, Lolo Soetoro, and then by his maternal grandparents. He lived in Indonesia with his mother and stepfather from the ages of six to ten years old, when he moved back to Hawaii to live with his mother's family. From that point on, he was raised by his maternal grandparents and attended Punahou Academy. Obama proved to be an adept student and excellent basketball player while at Punahou Academy from grades five through twelfth. He graduated in 1979.

While Obama's early years in Indonesia, where he attended a variety of schools of varying faiths, certainly proved valuable in teaching him the importance of diversity, it was undoubtedly his time in Hawaii that truly opened his eyes to racism and the struggles of growing up with a multiracial heritage. It was during this time that he first began to ponder the effect that social perceptions and preconceptions regarding race have upon all individuals. His passion for working for social equally was born, and would lead him to achieve the wide variety of accolades in his life to date.

Obama remained in Hawaii for the majority of his young adulthood. This is significant for a number of reasons, not the least of which is the fact that he was one of the very few African Americans on the island. He faced an uphill challenge when it came to understanding where to situate himself in the world according to his heritage. This difficulty was only compounded by the fact that his father had returned to Kenya in 1964 shortly after divorcing his mother, and later died in a car accident when Obama was 21 years old.

# COLLEGE YEARS

Once he had graduated from high school, Obama moved from Hawaii to Los Angeles in 1979. He attended Occidental College, a co-education and private liberal arts college. Located in Los Angeles in the neighborhood of Eagle Rock, the school was founded by clergy and other members from the Presbyterian Church in 1887. It is a distinguished school, and one of the oldest institutions of the liberal arts in the United States, and especially on the West Coast.

Occidental College is known to excel when it comes to community engagement, and this made it the perfect fit for Obama, who was already working on developing his community organization and engagement strategies. He attended the school for two years, during which time he called for the college to respond to the apartheid in South Africa by participating in its disinvestment. The speech he gave encouraging participation in the disinvestment in 1981 was his first public speech.

Before beginning his junior year of college – an undertaking that would occur at Columbia University – Obama decided to take a take trip visit his half-sister Maya and his mother in Indonesia in 1981. He spent a period of about three weeks in India, Pakistan, and Indonesia visiting with his family as well as the families of friends from college. When he returned to the States from the trip, Obama soon moved from Los Angeles to New York City, where he attended Columbia University for his junior and senior years of undergraduate study.

Obama took advantage of his time at Columbia University to read widely about international, political, and social issues. This helped make him particularly well informed for his major, political science with a concentration in international relations. He successfully completed his undergraduate degree and graduated in 1983, however he remained in New York City for another year working with Business International Group.

As an organizer for the global consulting firm, Obama gained proficiency in handling diverse situations.

# COMMUNITY ORGANIZER AND LAW SCHOOL

In 1984, Obama began working as a community organizer in the South Side of Chicago. This was his first immersive experience in the African American community that he had been unable to find in Hawaii, and he excelled with the work. Obama's main duty as a community organizer was launching the Developing Communities Project, a church-funded initiative developed to help residents band together and improve conditions within the community. More specifically, he worked to help organize those living in Altgeld Gardens in order to better lobby for much-needed improvements in the public housing project. He also worked to establish a college tutoring and preparatory program, a job training program, and even a tenants' rights organization. While he found that he was successful to a certain degree, Obama found it frustrating that he couldn't make significant progress without a law degree. He remained in the position from 1985 to 1988.

Immediately after leaving his position as a community organizer in Chicago, Obama traveled to Europe for the first time. He traveled for three weeks in Europe before moving on to Kenya. He spent five weeks there, meeting much of his paternal family for the first time and visiting the graves of his father and grandfather.

After returning from his travels, Obama began his time at Harvard Law School in 1988. His work as a student have been praised, and he excelled in the academic atmosphere. Aside from his classes, Obama also took part in a number of extra-curricular activities like the Harvard Law Review. He served the publication first as an editor, and then as president. His appointment as president of the journal was history-making and noted nationally as he was the first African American to achieve the position. He also worked as a research assistant to Laurence Tribe, a noted constitutional scholar, for two years. Obama spent his summers in Chicago working as an associate at Sidley Austin (1989) and Hopkins & Sutter (1990). It was during his first internship at Sidley Austin that he met his future wife, Michelle Robinson.

Success isn't about how much money you make, it's about the difference you make in people's lives.

-Michelle Obama

# CHICAGO LAW SCHOOL, MARRIAGE, & FIRST FORAY INTO POLITICS

Obama entered Chicago Law School in 1991 as a Visiting Law and Government Fellow. He spent his time working on his book, and then later taught constitutional law at the university for twelve years, 1992-2004. He directed Project Vote, a voter registration campaign in Illinois. Under his direction, the campaign managed to register 150,000 previously unregistered African American voters in the state. He was named as one of the "40 under Forty" individuals to watch by Crain's Chicago Business in 1993 as a direct result of his efforts in the campaign.

Also in 1993, Obama entered Davis, Miner, Barnhill & Galland, a law firm that specializes in neighbor and economic development and civil rights litigation. He served as first an associate and then of counsel over the course of eleven years. He also sat on the Woods Fund of Chicago board of directors from 1994 to 2002, concurrent with his work as an attorney, as well as on the board of directors of the Joyce Foundation.

Obama married Michelle Robinson in 1992 after courting for four years. They settled in Hyde Park, a middle-class and racially integrated neighborhood in Chicago. It was here that his daughters Malia (1998) and Natasha (2001) were born. In 1996, he was first elected to the Illinois Senate. While he initially faced a bit of hardship, he grew to cultivate bipartisan support for a wide variety of issues spanning from ethics to health care reform. He was elected to the U.S. Senate in 2004, and resigned from the State Senate accordingly. It would be remiss to neglect to mention Obama's keynote address in 2004 at the Democratic National Convention, which was incredibly successful and garnered quite a bit of attention and praise.

Obama was elected as the 44th President of the United States on November 4th, 2008. He won the popular vote at 52.9%, and was the first African American president. His victory speech was given in Grant Park in Chicago. He subsequently won the 2012 presidential election, securing the nomination on April 3, 2012. He was the first Democratic president to win the majority popular vote twice since Franklin D. Roosevelt.

# NOTABLE
# ACHIEVEMENTS

As the 44th President, Barack Obama has been responsible for a wide variety of achievements. He has championed causes for everything from healthcare reform to educational reform, and always dedicates as much time as possible to ensuring that the system is built in such a way that everyone has as equal a chance as anyone else to succeed. Below are a few of the achievements that will help comprise President Obama's legacy.

THE PATIENT PROTECTION
AND AFFORDABLE CARE ACT

Perhaps more commonly known as the Affordable Care Act (ACA), the PPACA was enacted on March 23, 2010. When combined with the Health Care and Education Reconciliation Act, the PPACA comprises one of the most significant overhauls to the healthcare system in the United States since 1965 when Medicare and Medicaid were passed. The act was designed to help provide affordable insurance and healthcare to Americans while simultaneously improving the level of care and adaptation of technology seen in hospitals.

Now broadly referred to as Obamacare, the PPACA faced many challenges from the start. There was a lot of opposition against the act and it has, unfortunately, seen many revisions and compromises. Its effectivity, however, cannot be questioned. Since the act went into effect, the number of uninsured individuals in the United States has dropped significantly. The overall cost of medical care has also been shown to be reduced, allowing more people to seek help without going into massive amounts of debt.

# CHILDREN'S HEALTH INSURANCE REAUTHORIZATION ACT

The CHIPRA is an expansion of the State Children's Health Insurance Program (SCHIP). SCIP was originally introduced by Edward Kennedy in 1997. It was created in order to expand healthcare coverage to children in order to help ensure that the nation's youth grow up as healthy as possible and has access to medical care regardless of family income. CHIPRA, signed in 2009 by President Obama, is an expansion of the program introduced by Kennedy. It further expands children's coverage as well as providing new incentives and programmatic options. Not only that, but the act also attempts to measure the kind of care that the children in question receive in order to ensure that they're experiencing the best care possible. It also aims to register children who qualify and need the coverage, but are currently unregistered. Children come first, and CHIPRA is one way to ensure that they remain insured and receive the care they need to stay healthy, even when their families go through hard times.

AMERICAN TAX PAYER
RELIEF ACT OF 2012

Enacted January 2 of 2013, the American Tax Payer Relief Act of 2012 seeks to close the vast income gap in the United States. One way to go about bridging the gap is by ensuring that individuals are taxed according to their income levels and overall wealth. A "one size fits all" approach doesn't help equalize the income gap in the slightest, and it makes sense that those who have more to spare should be asked to give more than a family or individual with nothing to spare whatsoever.

It is with accordance to that belief that the American Tax Payer Relief Act of 2012 was signed and enacted. The act makes permanent many tax breaks which were temporarily put in place by former president George W. Bush to help Americans recover after the first wave of the recession and real estate crash. In addition, the act ensures that higher tax rates stay in place for families and individuals in high income brackets rather than those in the very lowest income brackets.

# MATTHEW SHEPARD AND JAMES BYRD JR. HATE CRIMES PREVENTION ACT

Created as a direct reaction from the murders of James Byrd Jr. and Matthew Shepard. James Byrd Jr. was murdered in Texas in 1998 because of his race. Matthew Shepard was also murdered in 1998 in Wyoming because of his sexual orientation. Both men were tortured and suffered greatly throughout what can only be called hate crimes.

As a result, the Matthew Shepard and James Byrd Jr. Hate Crimes Prevention Act was created in order to expand the 1969 federal hate-crime law of the United States to remove certain prerequisites to classify a crime as a "hate crime" as well as to add sexual orientation, gender, disability, and gender identity as recognized motivators for hate crimes. Additionally, the act provided millions of dollars in funding to local and state agencies all over the United States to help pay for the investigation and prosecution of hate crimes. The act was signed into law on October 22, 2009, by President Obama.

# HOME AFFORDABLE
# MODIFICATION PROGRAM

---∽∞∾---

Towards the end of the early 2000s, the real estate market threw the United States into a tailspin with a subprime mortgage crisis. As a result, many Americans found themselves unable to pay for their homes and faced significant financial crisis. The Home Affordable Modification Program works to provide financial assistant to those homeowners who were hardest hit by the crisis. It was signed by Obama in 2009 and expires on December 31, 2016.

---∽∞∾---

# FDA FOOD SAFETY MODERNIZATION ACT

The idea that it's easier to play defense than it is offense is one that seems to reign true in a number of different industries. It was certainly true in the United States food industry, at the very least, where various agencies would frantically react to news of contaminated or otherwise unsafe food. The food industry played defense, in other words, and focused on damage control rather than working to ensure that no safety regulations were broken in the first place. The FDA Food Safety Modernization Act, signed in 2011 by President Obama, seeks to change this. Instead of waiting for a problem to occur, the FDA Food Safety Modernization Act seeks to shift the focus on prevention rather than reaction. This means that the FDA has new authority when it comes to regulating the way foods are processed, harvested, and grown. As a result, the number of contaminated food incidents has been reduced and the food industry has, in turn, reduced the expense of responded to these issues.

# DODD-FRANK WALL STREET REFORM
# AND CONSUMER PROTECTION ACT

More commonly known as simply "Dodd-Frank", the Dodd-Frank Wall Street Reform and Consumer Protection Act was a response to the Great Recession, the financial crisis that hit the United States during 2007 to 2010 as a result of irresponsible financial regulatory practices. The act sought to overhaul financial regulation in the United States, and in fact introduced the most significant changes in that industry since the reform that directly followed the Great Depression. It should be noted that the Dodd-Frank act was so extensive in its reform to regulations that it affected almost all parts of the United State's financial services industry as well as affecting all financial regulatory agencies on the federal level. The act is named after two members of Congress who championed the cause and worked hard to see it approved and signed into law. President Obama signed the act on July 21, 2010.

# LILLY LEDBETTER FAIR PAY ACT

The Civil Rights Act of 1964 remains one of the most important pieces of legislature ever enacted in the United States of America. It was the act that first put into law the idea that discrimination based on color, race, sex, national origin, or religion is unacceptable and illegal. It outlawed such behavior, in fact, and worked to end the unequal application of the requirements needed to register to vote as well as racial segregation in the workplace, in schools, and in public accommodations. While the act took a bit of time to fully enforce, its importance in the history of the United States is unquestionable. One thing that the Civil Rights Act of 1964 didn't ensure, however, was discriminatory pay. The Lilly Ledbetter Fair Pay Act works to rectify that oversight be ensuring that workers are given a fair amount of time to file a lawsuit for discriminatory pay. Previous law only gave 180 days from the date of the first paycheck affected by the discrimination to file suit, but the Lilly Ledbetter Fair Pay Act dictates that that period resets with every new paycheck that is affected. This was the very first bill that President Obama signed into law during the course of his presidency.

# CREDIT CARD ACCOUNTABILITY RESPONSIBILITY AND DISCLOSURE ACT OF 2009

Card card issuers are notorious for unexpected and unexplained fees that result in bills that are hundreds or thousands of dollars more than they should be. Sky-high and predatory interest rates and policies are another issue that many individuals seeking credit cards have experienced, and they can make paying off the debt seem nearly impossible. The Credit Card Accountability Responsibility and Disclosure Act of 2009, more commonly known as the Credit CARD Act, sought to overhaul the credit card industry and reform the regulations governing it. The purpose of this was to establish transparent and fair practices surrounding the extension of credit. It has helped end many predatory lending and credit extension practices that caused many Americans quite a bit of harm. President Obama signed the act in 2009.

# MEMORABLE QUOTES

On January 20, 2009, Barack Obama became the 44th President of the United States and first African American to hold this office. Along with his history of community organizing and dedication to civil rights, Obama is greatly admired for his powerful oratory. Drawing on intense study of America's founding documents and the legacies of American heroes such as former U.S. President Abraham Lincoln and the Reverend Dr. Martin Luther King, Jr., Obama has given numerous noteworthy and moving speeches. From the keynote address at the 2004 Democratic National Convention to his 2015 eulogy for the victims of the Charleston shooting, Obama reaches and moves audiences with personal narratives and sweeping visions for his country

Obama took a thoughtful, multifaceted approach toward building "a more perfect union." From student loans, education and economic stimulus to health care, marriage equality and consumer protection, Obama strove to deliver on his campaign promises of hope and change. His commitment to providing opportunity for every person to achieve his or her fullest potential earned Obama the 2009 Nobel Peace Prize only nine months after his first inauguration and won many significant gains for America in the eight years of Obama's two terms.

This book is a tribute to Obama's legacy. In the pages that follow, we honor President Obama as we reflect on several of his most memorable quotes

What has always united us – what has always driven our people; what drew my father to America's shores – is a set of ideals that speak to aspirations shared by all people: that we can live free from fear and free from want; that we can speak our minds and assemble with whomever we choose and worship as we please.

*Speech in Berlin, Germany, July 24th, 2008*

The future rewards those who press on. I don't have time to feel sorry for myself. I don't have time to complain. I'm going to press on.

*Congressional Black Congress Speech, September 24, 2011*

Now, as a nation, we don't promise equal outcomes, but we were founded on the idea everybody should have an equal opportunity to succeed. No matter who you are, what you look like, where you come from, you can make it. That's an essential promise of America. Where you start should not determine where you end up.

Focusing your life solely on making a buck shows a certain poverty of ambition. It asks too little of yourself. Because it's only when you hitch your wagon to something larger than yourself that you realize your true potential.

*Knox College Commencement Address, 2005*

There is not a liberal America and a conservative America—there is the United States of America. There is not a Black America and a White America and Latino America and Asian America—there's the United States of America.

We are the ones we've been waiting for. We are the change that we seek. We are the hope of those boys who have little; who've been told that they cannot have what they dream; that they cannot be what they imagine.

*Super Tuesday (2008)*

This is our moment. This is our time, to put our people back to work and open doors of opportunity for our kids; to restore prosperity and promote the cause of peace; to reclaim the American Dream and reaffirm that fundamental truth, that, out of many, we are one; that while we breathe, we hope. And where we are met with cynicism and doubts and those who tell us that we can't, we will respond with that timeless creed that sums up the spirit of a people: Yes, we can.

Clear-eyed, we can understand that there will be war, and still strive for peace. We can do that—for that is the story of human progress; that's the hope of all the world; and at this moment of challenge, that must be our work here on Earth.

*Nobel Peace Prize acceptance speech, 2009*

If you're walking down the right path and you're willing to keep walking, eventually you'll make progress.

*Barack Obama Speech on Race, March 18, 2008*

We did not come to fear the future. We came here to shape it.

In the end, if the people cannot trust their government to do the job for which it exists - to protect them and to promote their common welfare - all else is lost.

We've been warned against offering the people of this nation false hope. But in the unlikely story that is America, there has never been anything false about hope.

*New Hampshire Primary Speech, January 2008*

In the end, that's what this election is about. Do we participate in a politics of cynicism or a politics of hope?

*Democratic National Convention, 2004*

Money is not the only answer, but it makes a difference.

*Pre-Election Speech*

I don't oppose all wars. What I am opposed to is a dumb war. What I am opposed to is a rash war.

I don't care whether you're driving a hybrid or an SUV. If you're headed for a cliff, you have to change direction. That's what the American people called for in November, and that's what we intend to deliver.

*Speech to the House Democrats, February 2009*

The fact that we are here today to debate raising America's debt limit is a sign of leadership failure. America has a debt problem and a failure of leadership. Americans deserve better. I, therefore, intend to oppose the effort to increase America's debt.

That's the good thing about being president, I can do whatever I want.

We welcome the scrutiny of the world - because what you see in America is a country that has steadily worked to address our problems and make our union more perfect.

*Address to the United Nations General Assembly*

AFTER A CENTURY OF STRIVING
AFTER A YEAR OF DEBATE
AFTER A HISTORIC VOTE
Health Care Reform is no longer an unmet promise.

## IT IS THE LAW OF THE LAND.

We have an obligation and a responsibility to be investing in our students and our schools. We must make sure that people who have the grades, the desire and the will, but not the money, can still get the best education possible.

My fellow Americans, we are and always will be a nation of immigrants. We were strangers once, too.

*Announcing New Steps on Immigration, November 2014*

I consider it part of my responsibility as President of the United States to fight against negative stereotypes of Islam wherever they appear.

*Speech in Cairo, June 2009*

We need to internalize this idea of excellence. Not many folks spend a lot of time trying to be excellent.

Now the world will watch and remember what we do here

# WHAT WE DO WITH THIS MOMENT.

WILL WE EXTEND OUR HAND TO THE PEOPLE
IN THE FORGOTTEN CORNERS OF THIS WORLD
WHO YEARN FOR LIVES MARKED BY DIGNITY
AND OPPORTUNITY; BY SECURITY AND JUSTICE?

Will we lift the child in Bangladesh from poverty, shelter the refugee in Chad, **and** *banish the scourge of AIDS in our time?*

Your voice can change the world.

*Manassas, Virginia, Night Before the Election, November 2008*

# YES, WE CAN.

# PHOTO CREDIT

CPSIA information can be obtained
at www.ICGtesting.com
Printed in the USA
LVHW070419141220
672797LV00004BA/3

9 780998 235103